The Last Real Austins

1946 to 1959

Those were the days...

HB 7049

530 BTA

VELOCE

Other great books from Veloce –

Those Were The Days ... Series

Alpine Trials & Rallies 1910-1973 (Pfundner)
American 'Independent' Automakers – AMC to Willys 1945 to 1960 (Mort)
American Station Wagons – The Golden Era 1950-1975 (Mort)
American Trucks of the 1950s (Mort)
American Trucks of the 1960s (Mort)
American Woodies 1928-1953 (Mort)
Anglo-American Cars from the 1930s to the 1970s (Mort)
Austerity Motoring (Bobbitt)
Austins, The last real (Peck)
Brighton National Speed Trials (Gardiner)
British and European Trucks of the 1970s (Peck)
British Drag Racing – The early years (Pettitt)
British Lorries of the 1960s (Bobbitt)
British Touring Car Racing (Collins)
British Police Cars (Walker)
British Woodies (Peck)
Don Hayter's MGB Story – The birth of the MGB in MG's Abingdon Design & Development Office (Hayter)

Dune Buggy Phenomenon, The (Hale)
Dune Buggy Phenomenon Volume 2, The (Hale)
Endurance Racing at Silverstone in the 1970s & 1980s (Parker)
Hot Rod & Stock Car Racing in Britain in the 1980s (Neil)
Last Real Austins 1946-1959, The (Peck)
Mercedes-Benz Trucks (Peck)
MG's Abingdon Factory (Moylan)
Motor Racing at Brands Hatch in the Seventies (Parker)
Motor Racing at Brands Hatch in the Eighties (Parker)
Motor Racing at Crystal Palace (Collins)
Motor Racing at Goodwood in the Sixties (Gardiner)
Motor Racing at Nassau in the 1950s & 1960s (O'Neil)
Motor Racing at Oulton Park in the 1960s (McFadyen)
Motor Racing at Oulton Park in the 1970s (McFadyen)
Motor Racing at Thruxton in the 1970s (Grant-Braham)
Motor Racing at Thruxton in the 1980s (Grant-Braham)
Superprix – The Story of Birmingham Motor Race (Page & Collins)
Three Wheelers (Bobbitt)

www.veloce.co.uk

First published in April 2009 by Veloce Publishing Limited, Parkway Farm Business Park, Middle Farm Way, Poundbury, Dorchester, Dorset DT1 3AR England. Fax 01305 268864/e-mail info@veloce.co.uk/web www.veloce.co.uk or www.velocebooks.com. Reprinted March 2017.
ISBN: 978-1-787111-12-7 UPC: 6-36847-01112-3
Readers with ideas for automotive books, or books on other transport or related hobby subjects, are invited to write to the editorial director of Veloce Publishing at the above address.
British Library Cataloguing in Publication Data – A catalogue record for this book is available from the British Library. Typesetting, design and page make-up all by Veloce Publishing Ltd on Apple Mac. Printed and Bound by CPI Group (UK) Ltd, Croydon, CR04YY.

Contents

Acknowledgements & Introduction

Acknowledgements

This book would not have been possible without the help of numerous Austin owners, clubs and individuals around the world. There are far too many to mention them all individually, but I will list as many as I can here:

Roger Best
Mick Barnett
Paul Canty
Paddy Carpenter
Robin & Joan Crump
Peter Hackney
John Lakey
John Harris Lindsay
Norman Milne
Bill Munro
Jesse Patton

Bryan Peebles
Peter Ridgeway
Nick Savage
John Simpson
Mike Shackleton
Ron Short
Rob Stuart
Wayne Thompson
Matt Traxton
Bill Wilkman

In addition, I would like to acknowledge the involvement and contribution to my research activities of officers of the following organisations:
Austin Cambridge/Westminster Car Club
Austin Champ Owners Club
Austin Counties Car Club
Austin A30-A35 Owners Club
Austin A40 Farina Owners Club
Austin Healey Club
Austin Sheerline-Princess Owners Club
BMC J2/152 Register
Cambridge Oxford Owners Club
London Vintage Taxi Association
Police Vehicle Enthusiasts Club
Tilly Register
Vanden Plas Owners Club
Woodie Car Club

Introduction

My love affair with the outpourings of Longbridge began in 1965 when, after passing my driving test, I purchased a 1947 Austin Ten and then a 1949 A40 Devon within the space of a few months. Both were purchased for just a few pounds, and, whilst the Ten was sold on, sadly, the A40 was towed unceremoniously to the local scrapyard after the main engine bearings started rattling.

Over the following decades I and other family members owned a variety of Austins, including an A40 Somerset, A40 Cambridge, and an A40 Farina saloon. At one time I even owned an A55 Half Ton van, acquired for an ultimately unsuccessful business venture.

I rekindled my relationship with Austin when living in Los Angeles during the early 1990s whilst researching the failure of Austin in North America for *Classic Cars* magazine. Later, as an enthusiast, I returned an A40 dhc and an A70 Countryman to the UK for restoration.

In writing this book, just a handful of years after the Longbridge dynasty finally closed its doors and the new Chinese owners sent in the bulldozers, I offer it as a tribute to a marque that was unique in terms of innovation and quality, and also in its all-encompassing product range. After all, no other British auto maker can boast a range that included family, luxury and sports cars; off-roaders, military and special vehicles; limousines, taxicabs – and even light commercials – all within a single marque. Austin also had an enviable and unrivalled family of major associates, such as Vanden Plas, Jensen, Carbodies, and Healey.

The car production plant established by Herbert Austin in Longbridge in 1905 was destined to produce vehicles that would be revered the world over and much sought-after still decades later. From humble beginnings, the company grew quickly and dramatically, often as a result of employing innovative solutions to problems: for instance, during WWI, the Longbridge plant was contracted to manufacture armaments, yet there were no skilled tradesmen available to build new houses for the influx of munitions workers that the contract required. Herbert Austin resolved this problem by importing prefabricated bungalows from America to create the Austin Village, which still stands today as testament to the industrial might of Longbridge.

Despite an initial setback after WWI, which saw the company in the hands of the receivers, Austin continued to grow and prosper, largely due to the introduction of the Austin 7 in 1922. The company's increasing status

drew the attention of many within the industry, and, before acquiring Vauxhall, General Motors made a bid for the concern which was rejected, the legacy of which was to have some bearing on Austin's US export activities in post-war years.

Herbert Austin became Lord Austin of Longbridge in 1936, and, two years later, when he was 72, recruited Leonard Lord, the former works director of competitor Morris. Lord rose rapidly through the Austin hierarchy and became joint managing director in 1942, a year after Lord Austin died, then deputy chairman in 1943, and finally chairman in 1945.

Although initial plans for a merger with arch rival Morris collapsed in 1949, a statement outlining the terms of the amalgamation between Austin and the Nuffield Group was finally issued in November 1951. Some believe that the Austin A30 Seven was the last true Austin – the last Austin designed before the formation of BMC. However, it was many years before the bitter rivalry between Austin and Nuffield finally subsided.

So, Austin's management remained fiercely independent throughout the 1950s, and – while Austin and Morris may have shared engines during this period – most new Austins were designed and built in isolation of the Nuffield camp.

Colin Peck
Middlesex, England

The war years – a prelude to greatness

Austin's Longbridge factory had been contracted to produce armaments, aero engines, aircraft, and military trucks during WWI, so it was not surprising that much of the factory's capacity was turned over to supporting the war effort during the 1939-45 hostilities.

In addition to his role in orchestrating an automotive empire, Lord Austin was also appointed chairman of the British government-sponsored shadow factory scheme for aero engine production. So, as war clouds gathered over Europe during the late 1930s, he acquired the land across from the Longbridge factory at Cofton Hackett, where Austin's shadow factory was constructed.

The outbreak of war brought drastic changes to the car industry's production programmes, with everything ranging from trucks and tanks, to guns, ammunition – and even aircraft – now being built in those same factories. Austin was at the forefront of War Department vehicle production, turning out in total more than 90,000 trucks, which included ambulances, fire tenders, and 4x4 and 6x4 heavy-duty vehicles.

Whilst private car production was reduced, Austin manufactured limited numbers of Austin Eight and Ten variants for military use, and also produced small batches of the Twelve for use by regional police forces.

A militarised version of the Austin Eight tourer and batches of the Austin Ten saloon were also constructed for government use. However, one of the most numerous of Austin's WWII vehicles was the light utility truck based on the Ten. Developed in late 1939,

simultaneously with equivalent models from Hillman and Morris, the utility truck, or 'Tilly,' as it became widely known, was produced in a number of variants and saw service with the navy, army and airforce.

By the end of hostilities almost 29,000 Austin Tillys had been built. Despite being declared obsolete by the War Department as early as 1945, most continued in military service long after hostilities had ceased – many with other European nations, in addition to British forces. Following official demobilisation in the 1950s, Tillys were much sought-after by civilian buyers who acquired them at military disposal sales across the UK.

In addition to ammunition, mines, tanks, and, of course, vehicles, manufactured at the Longbridge plant, Cofton Hackett produced a variety of military planes during WWII. In fact, a total of 2855 aircraft – ranging from Fairey Battle fighter-bombers and Hawker Hurricane fighters to massive, four-engined Stirling and Lancaster bombers – were constructed by Austin's workforce. While some of the fighters could be directly flown out to assigned squadrons from the factory's small airfield, the bombers were too large and had to be transported by road in sections the few miles to the military airfield at Castle Bromwich, and also to Elmdon Airport which, today, is the site of Birmingham International Airport.

Sadly, Lord Austin did not live to see peace declared in Europe as he died on 23rd May 1941 after a short illness. He was succeeded as chairman by E L Payton who, in turn, was succeeded by Leonard Lord the following year, who was appointed both chairman and managing director.

In addition to building more than 29,000 utility trucks, during WWII, Austin's shadow factory at Cofton Hackett also constructed more than 320 Lancaster heavy bombers.

Pre-war carryovers and austerity

When car production resumed at Longbridge in August 1945, these four-door saloons – consisting of three basic models which could hardly be described as exciting – were, in effect, carry-overs from the pre-war range. The 900cc Austin Eight, introduced in 1939, and the 1125cc Austin New Ten featured an integrated chassis and body structure, whilst the 1535cc Twelve had a conventional chassis. All featured warmed-over versions of pre-war, side-valve engines.

However, all of this was destined to change within a short space of time. Austin had a new four cylinder, 2199cc overhead valve engine, which it had developed from a 1939 six cylinder engine designed for the company's new truck range. The four cylinder engine had originally been developed for installation in a 4x4 Jeep-style vehicle designed during WWII, but the war ended before the vehicle could leave the drawing board. So, this new engine was installed in the Twelve chassis and offered as the Austin Sixteen. Power was initially

Birmingham City Police Force Austin 10 goes out on patrol in May 1947. (Courtesy Police Vehicle Enthusiasts Club)

By putting the new 2199cc ohv four cylinder engine into the pre-war Twelve bodyshell, Austin created the Sixteen, which proved popular in numerous overseas markets. (Courtesy Jeff Nye)

rated at just 58bhp, but this was increased to 67bhp from April 1946.

Although car production at Longbridge had resumed, the post-war period in Britain was one of austerity and shortages. The country had accrued huge war debts, much of the industrial infrastructure lay in ruins, and there were shortfalls of everything from metal and fuel to basic food items.

However, an acute hunger for 'new' vehicles existed, so large numbers of surplus military vehicles were hastily re-commissioned by small garages and coachbuilding firms, with a variety of 'car-sized' bodies to meet this demand. Lea-Francis was one of the first British car makers to appreciate that a wood-framed utility body in the style of a shooting brake was the perfect short-term solution to both the shortage of steel for bodies and the need to produce as many cars as possible to meet demand.

It didn't take too long for Longbridge management to realise that offering a wooden-bodied utility, as it had done briefly in 1938-39, was a wise move, and so the company became one of the first British manufacturers to launch its own factory-approved Woodie, after tying up a deal

with Papworth Industries in Cambridgeshire for the construction of 250 Austin Sixteen shooting brakes.

Coachbuilding officially began at Papworth in 1947 after Papworth's sales manager visited Austin's Longbridge works, where he learnt that the company was planning to build a number of shooting brakes. Papworth's head carpenter had worked for the General Omnibus Company after the First World War, and his experience helped Papworth win the contract to build what was to become the Sixteen BW1 Countryman.

It was the first contract that the Cambridgeshire company had won for the construction of vehicle bodies, though was destined not to be its last. The 250 Sixteen Countryman shooting brakes were produced to such a high standard, and on time, that an order was placed for a further 250.

Longbridge awarded 2 contracts for a total of 500 wooden shooting brake bodies to Papworth Industries for what was to become the Austin Sixteen Countryman.

Export or die

Austin had been fortunate in that it had been able to resume post-war production before other British auto makers, and it was financially healthy, thanks to substantial War Department contracts. So, in 1945, under Len Lord's leadership, the Austin board sanctioned a £1million investment in a modernisation programme.

The future looked exceedingly bright for Austin, just as long as it concentrated on building vehicles for export. In Britain in the period immediately after WWII, new cars could only be purchased by priority customers who had obtained a purchasing certificate from the Ministry of War Transport. Despite red tape, petrol rationing, massive prices increases, and an extremely long wait for delivery – with some buyers quoted delivery times of up to four years – demand for cars on the home market was strong.

The reason for the long delivery times was because Britain had amassed huge war debts during the war, particularly in North America, and so exports were crucial to help the country achieve some sort of economic stability and incoming credit with which to purchase food and raw materials. Therefore, the British government gave the auto industry strict instructions to prioritise delivery of vehicles for export, or risk having its supply of raw materials – such as steel and coal for furnaces – withdrawn. In essence, Austin had to export the majority of its new cars in order to stay in business.

Lord was determined that Austin would be competitive in key export markets, and embarked on a thorough modernisation of Longbridge, which resulted in the construction of a state-of-the-art assembly building, the envy of British and foreign motor manufacturers for many years. In fact, the team at Longbridge was so committed to modernisation that when suppliers were reluctant to design and build the new machines and tools that Austin required, Longbridge took the view that not only would it design and build motor cars, but also have its workforce design and build the very machines required to make them!

However, Austin's export drive could only really begin in earnest with the launch of a totally new post-war range of cars. The company had found no great demand for 1939-designed cars, so the race was on to build a distinctive modern range of vehicles.

In May of 1947, Lord sailed to the US to study market conditions – returning in August that year to form subsidiary companies in both the US and Canada. He also took with him a number of mysterious crates, which contained the first pre-production models of the new A40 four-door Devon and the two-door Dorset, plus a Sheerline and a Princess.

The A40 Devon was launched in the US in 1947. Initial sales were brisk, due to a frustrated demand for new cars, and even today the cars have a strong following amongst North American enthusiasts. Tom McCahill, from *Mechanix Illustrated* – often dubbed 'The voice of motoring' in post-war America – was there on the docks to greet the cars, and got straight to the point in reporting that: "These new Austins are built especially for the American trade, and if I may rudely suggest, the American dollar."

Lord's timing was perfect, as the American market had been starved of new cars for four years, although,

The A40 Devon was launched in the US in 1947. Sales were initially brisk, due to a frustrated demand for new cars. Today, the car has a strong following amongst North American enthusiasts.

unlike in Britain, there were no long waiting lists or restrictions on purchase. In addition, America's Big Three auto makers – Ford, GM, and Chrysler – initially offered warmed-over pre-war designs only, and it was not until 1949 that their new designs came on-stream. Austin had brand new, technologically-advanced designs that were available, although the backlog of demand would not last for ever. As a result of this bold move Len Lord returned to Longbridge with dealer orders worth millions of pounds, and Austin looked set to become a key player in the North American auto industry.

A40s were advertised in America as achieving 30mpg, with a 30 per cent fuel saving compared to the average American car. Adverts also highlighted "the finest craftsmanship of England's largest builder of motor cars" and "the last word in motor car perfection," but were more directly misleading in how the physical size of the cars were represented, some adverts using artwork that appeared stretched in order to make the small Austins appear closer to the 15-18 feet length of the average Chevrolet or Plymouth of the day.

Austin also had sales slogans that claimed the A40 was a "family-sized car with speed and power to spare" which, to most American buyers, meant a six-seater with a six or eight cylinder engine. If Austin had chosen to introduce the A70 Hampshire in the US, with its slightly larger passenger cabin and 80mph top speed, then this model might have gone some way toward giving credence to this claim. However, it is rumoured that GM stated that, whilst it would not object to the A40s entering the American market, it would be most unhappy if Austin also brought in the A70. So it didn't!

Austin even produced a special booklet for those American drivers not used to small four cylinder engines,

Members of the Four Cylinder Club in Southern California brought a collection of Austins to a club gathering in the early 1950s. (Courtesy Bill Wilkman)

An early chrome grille A40 pickup at Fisherman's Wharf, San Francisco.

which aimed to educate them about how to extract the most power from the 40bhp Austin engine by using several hundred rpm more than would normally be used on big-engined American cars.

However, whilst the A40 was acceptable by UK standards of the day, it was considered very 'busy' at speed compared with American six- and eight-cylinder motors, and, with its low rear axle ratio, the 1200cc motor had to work hard to maintain the 60mph cruising speed that was common on wide open North America highways.

Within a year of the A40's launch around 60,000 examples had rolled off the production lines at Longbridge, approximately 10,000 cars going to the US, and only 1000 or so retained for privileged home market buyers.

Government policy for 1948 was increasingly tough on British motor manufacturers, and early in the year it was announced that only those manufacturers which were exporting 75 per cent of their production (50 per cent previously) would receive an allocation of steel. In addition, the government wanted to increase UK car production by more than 50 per cent over 1947 output, and set a year-end target of 475,000 cars.

However, although more cars were produced than in the previous year, the combined British motor industry managed to produce only 334,815 cars, an amazing 226,911 of which were exported.

Austin's early efforts were truly exceptional, exporting 60 per cent of its production and far out-performing rivals such as Morris or Rootes. During March 1948, the company broke all previous export records when 5722 vehicles, worth £2 million, left Longbridge. Of the 1200 cars sent to America that month by all British manufacturers, 1053 were Austins.

In fact, Austin did so well in earning US dollars – which helped to put food on tables across Britain – that the British Government issued a statement to the effect that Austin's export efforts with the A40 had earned more dollars for Britain than any other single product of any type.

By the end of 1948, the New York-based Austin Motor Export Corporation Ltd had established a network of 90 dealers across the US, including 18 in the important New York state region and six in California. Dealers were selected on an exclusive basis as the company considered there to be great prestige associated with selling Austin cars.

At the time Austin was still convinced that fuel economy was a major selling tool – as it was in other markets – and so a special economy run was undertaken in 1950. Under the supervision of the American Automobile Association, a Devon saloon averaged 33.34 miles per US gallon on the 514 mile New York to Toronto run, which, at that time, equated to 112 miles for just one dollar!

However, despite US sales of the A40 peaking at 10,000 units in 1948, Austin's advances into America were not proving profitable, Lord stating in 1949 that Austin was actually selling cars in the US at less than the cost of production. This was a difficult situation because, by the time that the A40s had travelled 3000 miles from Birmingham to New York, and then onward to dealers, their showroom price actually made them more expensive than home-produced offerings.

At US $1475 for a two-door Dorset and $1575 for a Devon, home-built competitors such as the 1948 Ford Super Deluxe with V8 power, selling for $1440 and the

Fred Deeley Motors, an Austin dealership in Vancouver, sponsored this major exhibition of Longbridge products at the Seaforth Armouries in Vancouver in 1951. (Courtesy Old English Car Club of Canada)

The steel-bodied A40 Countryman proved popular in a variety of export markets. (Courtesy Mike Minter)

General Motors thoroughly examined the A40 and declared that it would not make a political fuss about imported cars if Austin stuck to importing only the small A40s and the A90 Atlantic.

six cylinder Chevrolet Stylemaster at just $1371 gave the four-cylinder Austins a lot to compete with. Even the brand new four-door Studebaker – the first US manufactured post-war design – could undercut the Devon by $100.

Things went a little better for Austin in Canada, where the newly-formed Austin Motor Company (Canada) Ltd acquired a disused factory in Hamilton, Ontario, for the assembly of CKD kits from Britain, and announced plans to build 500 cars a week the following year.

In fact, Austin was so sure of itself in Canada that it took space at the Ontario Auto Show held in August 1948, and exhibited the newly-launched A70 Hampshire alongside the even newer A90 Atlantic, a month before the A90 was officially launched in Britain. Overall, Canada proved a much better outlet for Austin and, in 1950, more than 23,000 cars were sold there, compared with US sales of just 4800.

While both the A70 and A90 had been designed for export, only the Atlantic was destined to be sold in

the US. General Motors thoroughly examined the A40s and declared that they would not make a political fuss about imported cars if Austin stuck to importing only the small A40s and the Atlantic. Of course, neither model competed with anything that GM was building at the time.

The burgeoning North American sports car market appealed to the Austin board, so it designed the bold, if not radical, A90 Atlantic specifically for that market.

While fuel economy had been the basis for one plan of attack, the burgeoning North American sports car market also appealed to the Austin board, and so it designed the bold, if not radical, A90 Atlantic specifically for that market. It was futuristically streamlined, had a column-mounted gear lever and a top speed of 95mph.

In 1952 an A90 Atlantic accompanied three London Transport double-decker buses on a tour of the US and Canada promoting Britain and its products. While the buses survived the trip and returned to passenger service in London, sadly, the A90 was involved in an accident and damaged beyond repair. (Courtesy www.stilltimecollection.co.uk)

The A40 Devon saloon and the A40 Sports helped establish the Austin brand in North America.

In fact, it had everything that Austin perceived the American buyer would want except – of course – a longer wheelbase and a V8 engine!

Austin's public relations officer, Alan Hess, took an A90 to the Indianapolis Speedway and managed to set some 63 new records, including a record-breaking 11,850 miles at an average speed of 70.68mph. However, despite a huge advertising campaign to promote the Atlantic's achievements, sales were slow. Len Lord later moaned "What benefit have we got in sales in America? I'm afraid that answer is none – the response to the A90 has been disappointing."

A hard top 'Sports sedan' version of the A90 was introduced in 1949 but failed to attract many customers.

Everything about the American market was beginning to disappoint Lord, who had concentrated his maximum export effort there. Sales were falling away fast, and even those that remained were unprofitable.

During the period June-August 1948, some 7000 Austins were sent to the US. In the same period in 1949 exports there had fallen to just 460. However, while Austin began to accept the fact that American buyers were not ready to jump into four-cylinder cars in their thousands, there was a slight increase in acceptance of economy cars.

In 1950, Nash introduced its bulbous Rambler, powered by an 82bhp side-valve six and selling for an amazingly low $1173, and there was also growing competition in the US from arch rival Morris with its compact Minor. However, the confusion arising from rumours of an impending merger between Morris and Austin didn't exactly help sales of Longbridge products ...

In comparison to North America, Australia was a good market for Austin, where it outsold all other cars imported in 1949 by a margin of 5000 vehicles. The A40 proved a winner with 18,000 finding

Left: In the rush to launch the Atlantic in Australia, the A90 demonstrator was inadvertently sold. So this car, believed to be prototype number 5, was flown from the UK in time for the 1949 Melbourne motor show. (Courtesy Peter Hackney)

Lord Howe Island, widely regarded as one of the most beautiful in the Pacific, is the closest island getaway to Sydney, Australia. One of the few vehicles to make it there was this A40 'ute, purchased second-hand by Frank Robbins in 1958 and shipped to the island to be used as a taxi. Getting such vehicles ashore was a precarious task, and the A40 had to be craned over the side of a ship onto a ramp made from two lighters lashed together. Once the lighters were beached the A40 had to be rolled ashore down a makeshift ramp, where it was fitted with seats and used to run islanders to the cinema two nights a week. (Courtesy J David Jones)

customers in 1951, helping to make it the second most popular car sold in Australia behind the market-leading Holden. Austin's antipodean success allowed the largest Austin distributor, Larke Hoskins of Sydney, to make a reported profit of £1 million for the year.

While Austin had produced an open tourer version of the pre-war Eight, the post-war line-up did not include this model. A prototype A40 tourer was built in Britain to establish how many of the existing panels could be used for such a car, but never went into production in the home market.

However, the tourer concept was successfully put

The A40 Tourer was built locally in Australia by a number of Austin assemblers. This example is believed to be rolling off the assembly line at Pressed Motor Corporation in Enfield, near Sydney. (Courtesy John Lindsay)

into production in Australia, where a large number of A40-based, two-door tourers were bodied by Austin assembly plants in Sydney and Melbourne. Dominium Motors, Austin's distributor in Brisbane, also produced a similar tourer. In addition to the cars being assembled from CKD at six plants across Australia, Austin was also assembling Austins in New Zealand, Ireland, and throughout South America.

By mid-1950, Austin was claiming to have exported 10,000 vehicles to Belgium since the end of the war, and, by the end of the year, had produced its 250,000th A40, four out of five of which were exports. By this time, Britain had become the world's largest exporter, with Austin playing a pivotal role in this momentous achievement.

News came in 1951 that Austin and Morris were planning to merge to form BMC Australia. The scene appeared set for Austin and Morris to enjoy one of the biggest car booms ever, as in just 20 years Australia's vehicle population had rocketed from 1.4 to 5 million. There were enormous profits to be made in the Australian car industry, though not, unfortunately, by Austin or BMC Australia.

The management of BMC Australia was made up of locals who ran the business and the bean counters in Longbridge who owned it. BMCA was never allowed to forget that it was a subsidiary of a British firm, and its main job was to buy from Britain and sell to Australia, which meant that cars specifically designed to take on the market-leading Holden light sixes never got off the drawing boards. As a result of this blinkered outlook, BMCA's market share withered from the combined 30.7 per cent it enjoyed in 1951 to just 6 per cent within 20 years.

Export and die! This A40 Countryman was one of many exported to Chile before ending its days in the proverbial barn. (Courtesy Lars Sorenson)

Visit Veloce on the web: www.veloce.co.uk
Information on all books • New book news • Special offers • Gift vouchers • Forum

21

Small family cars

Austin's most memorable car, the humble Austin Seven, had been replaced by the Austin Eight prior to the outbreak of war in Europe in 1939. Although the Eight was reincarnated post-war, it was itself replaced – along with the Ten – by the brand new A40 saloons in 1947.

As the A40s were altogether larger than the Eight, Austin's model range was initially bereft of an economy-sized car. Whilst this omission had been foreseen in 1946, there was a more pressing and immediate need to focus on North American exports to generate dollars that would help pay off Britain's huge war debts.

The bean counters at Longbridge knew that a small Austin was hardly going to beget many US or Canadian sales, so the project was held on the drawing board

Despite a radical styling concept developed for the A30 by Raymond Loewy studios, the A30 Seven was restyled by Austin's head stylist to give it a 'family' resemblance to the A70 Hereford, and the soon-to-be-launched A40 Somerset.

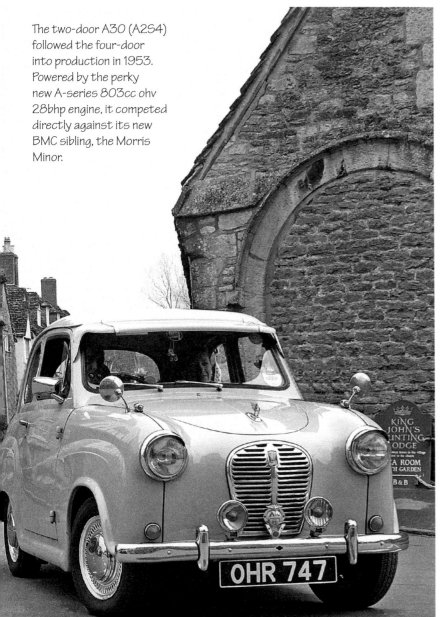

The two-door A30 (A2S4) followed the four-door into production in 1953. Powered by the perky new A-series 803cc ohv 28bhp engine, it competed directly against its new BMC sibling, the Morris Minor.

awaiting the right moment to be scheduled for production. That moment came in 1949 after the collapse of Len Lord's plans to merge with Morris.

With the merger deal in ruins, Austin urgently needed a rival to the Morris Minor, which had proven a sales success for the Cowley-based firm since its launch a year earlier. Ironically, by the time the new Austin was launched as the A30 Seven at the 1951 London Motor Show, the merger with Morris was finally sealed, with the new baby Austin's engine destined to also power the rival Morris Minor!

Styling of the A30 Seven was initially conceived by Bob Koto, a designer from Raymond Loewy studios. A full-sized clay model, with exceptional styling for a small car, was produced, but, as a result of cost-cutting, some 4½ inches were chopped off the back, and it was ignominiously restyled by Austin's head stylist, Dick Burzi, to give it a 'family resemblance' to the new A70 Hereford and the soon-to-be launched A40 Somerset.

In engineering terms the new car was a radical departure for Austin as it was a truly 'chassisless car' – not only a first for Longbridge, but for the British car industry generally. Even its engine was a trendsetter as the industry norm for small cars at the time was a side-valve powerplant, as was the case with

Legendary London-based Austin dealer Car Mart could always be counted on to put on a great display of Austins. This brand new A35 two-door is seen sharing a nautical theme with one of the earliest jet-skis. (Courtesy www.stilltimecollection.co.uk)

the rival Minor. The diminutive Austin was powered by a brand new 803cc, overhead valve engine providing 28bhp, developed from the design of the A40 1200cc engine, and later to be known as the BMC A-series.

Under the old RAC horsepower rating the new car was technically an Eight, but, ever keen to emulate some of the popularity of the iconic pre-war Seven, the new baby Austin was launched as the A30 Seven at the October 1951 London Motor Show. With a launch price of £100 less than the rival Morris Minor, the A30 was priced to secure buyers and was so successful that it racked up sales of more than 250,000 vehicles.

On the road, the new baby Austins really stood out, not least because they were the narrowest cars you could buy at the time, and drew lots of journalistic comparisons with the Morris Minor. The A30 was initially only available as a four-door saloon (AS3), although a prototype convertible was built in 1951, but not put into production. A two-door (A2S4) version had been planned from the outset, which eventually went into production in 1953, followed a year later by the 5cwt van (AV4) and the Countryman estate car (AP4).

The A30 was produced until October 1956 when it was replaced by the much improved A35. A painted grille

A painted grille, flashing indicators and bigger back window were some of the external improvements found on the A35 launched in October 1956 in both two- and four-door variants.

Just 497 of the 'tax dodge' A35 pickups slipped out of Longbridge before the British government slapped purchase tax on them, effectively causing Austin to cancel production.

Production of both the A35 Countryman and A35 van carried on well into the 1960s, long after the cars had been discontinued.

with chrome surround, flashing indicators, and bigger rear window on the two-door (A2S5) and four-door (AS5) saloons, were the only external improvements, though lurking beneath the bonnet was a new 948cc, A-series engine that cranked out 34bhp.

A new gearbox, plus a higher ratio back axle, gave the new car much improved high speed cruising ability, and a top speed almost 10mph faster than that of its predecessor.

The A35 Countryman was a versatile vehicle that could easily carry people or goods.

Styled by Italian designer Pinin Farina, the new small Austin was revolutionary in that it was the first mass-produced British car to have the hatchback styling of today.

Both van and Countryman variants were built, as well as the short-lived pickup truck, which was essentially intended as a tax-dodge, designed to function as a two-seater car on which no purchase tax was levied, due to its classification as a commercial vehicle. However, a miniscule rear load space made it a most impractical load carrier, and immediately the British Government decided that it was not 'technically' a real commercial vehicle and therefore liable to purchase tax. This decision effectively sounded the death knell for the pickup and it was deleted from the A35 range at the end of 1957 after just 497 had been sold.

While the A35 van and Countryman were to remain in production until well into the 1960s, the arrival of the square-set A40 during 1958 heralded not only a new era for small Austin cars, but also signalled the demise of the A35 saloons, which were deleted early the following year so that production space at Longbridge could be used for the soon-to-be-launched Mini.

Styled by Italian designer Pinin Farina, the new A40 was revolutionary in that it was the first mass-produced British car to have the hatchback styling of today. It was powered by the same 948cc engine as the A35, yet was to be available as a two-door only, unlike its predecessor. Both Jensen and Vanden Plas were commissioned to build a series of prototype convertibles based on the A40, but neither made it into production.

A40 CKD kits were assembled in Australia, New Zealand, Mexico, South Africa, Holland, Belgium and Ireland, while the A40 in Norway and Sweden was known as the A40 Futura. The car was also marketed in the US where it was advertised as "One of the most stylish little cars in the US today" and "Exciting to drive."

Curiously, at a time when BMC was about to enter the era of 'badge engineering' with its 1.5 litre Farina-designed, family-sized cars and soon-to-be-introduced front-wheel-drive models, there wasn't a Morris version of the A40, meaning that the Morris Minor remained in production for another 13 years.

Family cars

Austin ceased production of its pre-war-designed Eight and Ten saloons in 1947, replacing them with the 'new Ten:' the A40. Whereas previous model types were based on the historic RAC horsepower rating, the new Austins set a trend by using the brake horsepower rating (bhp) – hence the 40bhp Devon (GS2) and Dorset (G2S2) range became the A40.

The A40s were new from end to end, including chassis, body, and the sturdy 1200cc, ohv four cylinder engine, which proved very reliable. Producing 40bhp at 4300rpm, the ohv unit was more efficient and more powerful than the old 1125cc side-valve engine that it superceded.

The A40s were the first contemporary 'family' cars

The four-door Austin A40 Devon was introduced in 1947 and remained in production until 1952 when it was replaced by the A40 Somerset.

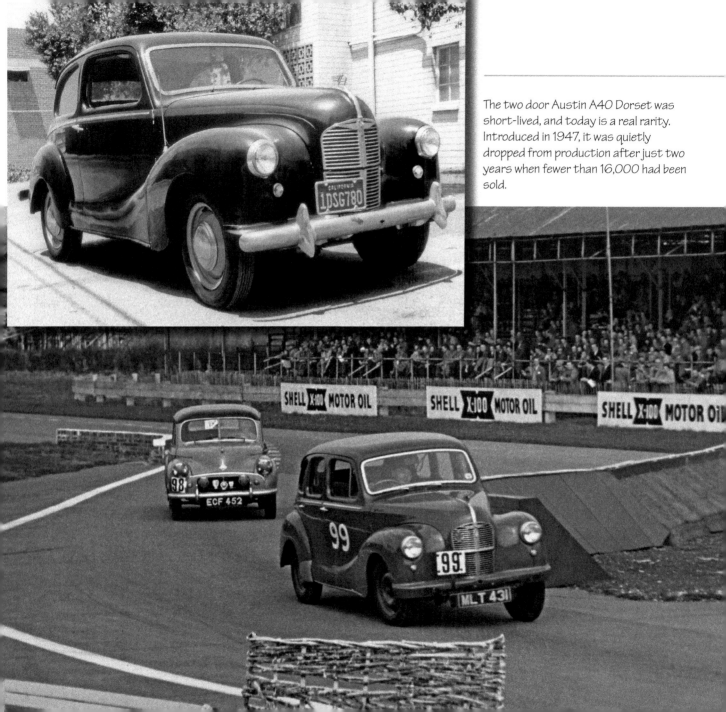

The two door Austin A40 Dorset was short-lived, and today is a real rarity. Introduced in 1947, it was quietly dropped from production after just two years when fewer than 16,000 had been sold.

to be launched in post-war Britain. In addition to a brand new ohv motor, the chassis was also new and featured independent front suspension – an innovation for Austin. By comparison, the Vauxhall Wyvern launched in 1948 was basically a pre-war Vauxhall 10 H-body with new front and rear ends grafted on, while Hillman's first truly new design wasn't launched until 1949, and even that had an antiquated side-valve engine.

The A40s were available in bright new colours, an option probably lost on the British public as, with the main bulk of production destined for export markets, realistically there was little chance of buying one in *any* colour. In fact, such was the clamour to export that, of the first 30,000 A40s built, only 1000 became available on the home market.

Initially, the bulk of A40 production went to North America and Canada where it neatly filled a void in North American car manufacturing capability. The Commonwealth countries were also targeted by Austin, and, by 1951, the A40 was the second most popular car sold in Australia with a 16.6 per cent market share compared with GM Holden's 23 per cent and Morris' 13.8 per cent.

The two-door A40 Dorset was short-lived, however, and was quietly dropped from production just two years after its introduction: fewer than 16,000 were built

Left: A salesman's car during the week and a racer at the weekend! The late RCC Palmer used this A40 Devon as a company car during the week and then raced it at weekends. Fitted with modified suspension, twin SU carbs, and brake cooling aids, the car is seen here hurtling through the legendary chicane at Goodwood.
(Courtesy Michael Davidson)

compared with almost 275,000 Devons. In fact, very few Dorsets were ever sold in Britain as the model had been taken off the home market in September 1948: thus, today, the A40 Dorset is one of the rarest of the surviving Austins.

Whilst the anomaly that was the pre-war-designed Sixteen soldiered on until 1949, work on its replacement – the A70 Hampshire (BS2) – had begun in 1947 using the six-light bodyshell of the new A40 Devon. Sir John Black, deputy chairman and managing director of the Standard Motor Company, was apparently the inspiration behind the new car when he announced his intention to introduce the Standard Vanguard long before the company could actually build it. So Len Lord arranged to visit Black, who showed him the car, and they discussed strategies for their various new models.

Lord returned to Longbridge with instructions to put the 2.2 litre engine from the Sixteen into the Devon chassis, to compete with the Vanguard. The A40 chassis was lengthened and widened by four inches and three prototypes were produced. A purpose-built chassis was eventually designed for production versions.

Announced in September 1948, the new A70 was described as being 'additional' to the Sixteen and so sold alongside its predecessor for a short while, which it undercut by £75. Powered by the lusty 2199cc ohv engine, and with a sleek new body based on a widened A40 Devon bodyshell, the 68bhp Hampshire had a top speed well in excess of 80mph, and could almost be considered a 'sports saloon' by today's standards.

The A70 had independent front suspension, a trendy column-mounted gear lever, and hydro-mechanical brakes; the rear wheels were hidden behind detachable spats to emphasise its streamlined look.

The introduction of the Standard Vanguard by Sir John Black, deputy chairman and managing director of the Standard Motor Company, was apparently the inspiration behind the A70 Hampshire, which was to finally replace the Austin 16 in 1949.
(Courtesy www.stilltimecollection.co.uk)

Announced in September 1948, the new A70 was described as 'additional' to the Sixteen, and so sold alongside its predecessor for a short while, which it undercut by £75.

Described by *The Autocar* magazine as having "a smart but not exaggerated modern appearance," the Hampshire saloon proved extremely popular with British police forces – some even purchased the wooden-bodied BW3 Countryman estate car, just over 900 of which were built for Austin by Papworth Industries between 1949 and 1950.

In addition to the Countryman version, a small number of Hampshire convertibles were built by at least two different coachbuilders. The lines of both versions aped the Longbridge-built Atlantic, and would have undoubtedly been more expensive to build so, sadly, disappeared into oblivion all too quickly.

While the A40 Devon enjoyed a five year production run, its big brother, the Hampshire, was built for just two years, being replaced by the A70 Hereford, which was launched in October 1950 at the London Earls Court Motor Show.

During testing in May 1951, the new A70 was hailed by *The Motor* as "Bigger and better than the previous Hampshire," and, indeed, did have a three inch longer wheelbase in an effort to overcome the rear legroom shortcomings of its predecessor. However, overseas journalists were more candid in their opinions of the car's styling, some referring to the Hereford as the first of the 'toby jugs.' The A70's design was indeed evident in both the A30 Seven and the A40 Somerset which followed it into production.

Its styling was certainly old school when compared with the slab-sided monocoque Ford

With a top speed of more than 80mph, the A70 proved popular with a number of British police forces. These two A70s were part of the all-Austin fleet of patrol cars operated by Dorset police. (Courtesy Dorset Police)

Surrey police also used A70 patrol cars, this example accompanied by stern-faced officers. (Courtesy Surrey police)

Left: Just over 900 of these wooden-bodied A70 Hampshire Countryman shooting brakes were built for Austin by Papworth Industries of Cambridgeshire.

This sleek A70 Hampshire convertible was bodied by an unknown coachbuilder, and has different lines to the Dutch-built A70 convertibles shown at the 1950 Amsterdam Show. Curiously, the car is RHD and has what appears to be flashing indicators at the front.

Here's a car that pays you a bonus every year!

AUSTIN A70 HEREFORD
A remarkable car. Family saloon that cruises around 65 ; takes 5/6 people in restful, smooth comfort for very long distances. Like all Austins the Hereford has safety glass windows throughout. £596 plus £249 . 9 . 2 Purchase Tax. Hide seats, heater, radio and clock extra.

AN AUSTIN gives you all the performance you could want. You get styling and equipment and finish as good as they can be made. And you get that little bit more for your gallon.

But you get something extra, and you get it free. You get Dependability. And Dependability means that given petrol, oil and water your Austin goes on and on and on. Your repair bills are few and far between. Each year your Austin saves you money, saves you worry and gives you the very best of motoring.

Taking your Austin abroad this year ?
Take advantage of the Austin Owners' Continental Touring Scheme

In addition to your normal travel allowance you can buy Austin Repair Vouchers in the U.K. to a value of £10, £25 or £50. They are valid for repairs and replacements at Austin Dealers or authorised garages on the Continent. When you return to the U.K., unused vouchers will be cashed. Touring kits containing invaluable equipment can also be borrowed for a nominal charge.
Ask your Austin Dealer for complete details

AUSTIN – you can depend on it!

THE AUSTIN MOTOR COMPANY LIMITED • LONGBRIDGE • BIRMINGHAM

The days of using artist's impressions were almost over when this A70 Hereford advertisement appeared in 1953.

Consuls and Zephyrs that arrived on the market a few months later, along with the E-series Vauxhall Wyverns and Veloxes. Whereas both Ford and GM products had taken styling cues from their American parents, Austin stuck with more traditional designs, which may well have contributed to plummeting sales in North America.

In order to boost overseas sales of the Hereford, Carbodies was asked to build a drophead coupé version (dhc). Austin was already involved with Carbodies in the production of the FX3 taxicab, and, having examined the

Austin struck a deal with Carbodies to build a convertible version of the A70 Hereford. This, however, resulted in just 266 BD3 drophead coupés being built, with some 186 sold on the home market. Today, it is one of the rarest of Austins with just a handful of known survivors.

Coventry-based coachbuilder's handiwork in a stylish dhc version of the then-new Hillman Minx phase III in 1948, it was a natural candidate to build a limited production run to test the market.

The deal, however, resulted in just 266 BD3 coupés being built, with some 186 sold on the home market. Today, the model is one of the rarest Austins, with just a handful of known survivors, and even fewer in roadworthy condition.

With the introduction of the Hereford, Papworth Industries was once again given a contract to build a wood-framed Countryman version. Production began in earnest in 1951 of the last Longbridge-approved 'woodies;' some 1550 were built at the Papworth Everard works between 1951 and 1954.

Just six months before production of the A40 Devon came to an end in 1952, a revised version (GS3) was introduced with a column gear change, a new dashboard and steering wheel, and fully hydraulic brakes to replace the previous hydro-mechanical setup. These improvements were in anticipation of the arrival of a new A40 body style, the Somerset, which appeared in the spring of 1952.

By 1951, the Devon had contended with increasing

Following the success of the A70 Hampshire Countryman, Austin contracted Papworth Industries to build more than 1500 Hereford-based Countryman shooting brakes. (Courtesy Peter Bull)

Powered by a 1200cc, four cylinder ohv engine, which had been tweaked to produce 42bhp by employing the same cylinder head as that fitted to the A40 Sports, the Somerset was an admirable successor to the Devon.

competition on the home market from cars such as the sleek new Ford Consul and the smaller Morris Minor, so the new A40 was a brave step toward reversing the sales slide. The Somerset was both the last new Austin to bear the name of an English county, and the last

The A40 Somerset sold well in Canada, but could not achieve the sales success of the earlier Devon and Dorset models. (Courtesy Dave Golding)

new Austin range to be built with a separate body and chassis.

Looking like a scaled-down version of the A70 Hereford – in fact, it used the same doors – the Somerset continued the 'toby jug' theme. Somehow, the bodywork seemed more in proportion, and better-suited, to the new smaller Austin than the longer and wider Hereford. Having had to halt production of the two-door Dorset due to lack of demand, Austin offered the Somerset only as a four-door.

Powered by a 1200cc, four-cylinder ohv engine, tweaked to produce 42bhp by employing the same cylinder head as that fitted to the A40 Sports, the Somerset was an admirable successor to the Devon. However, it was not destined to sell in such large numbers as, by the time it was launched, competition was a lot stiffer.

Keen to rectify the sales shortcomings of the Jensen-bodied A40 Sports, Austin added a two-door drophead coupé to the Somerset range, contracting Carbodies to build a convertible similar to the A70 drophead already in production. Some 7243 examples were built over a two year period, with most of the early production destined for North America.

An interesting deal was struck between Austin and Nissan in Japan, which needed help in updating its factories. As a result, Somersets were built under licence in Japan, and were instrumental in helping Nissan become the major force it is today. When the Somerset was phased out at the end of 1954, the new cars that followed were not only new from bumper to bumper, but also meant that Longbridge switched completely to monocoque construction, following the success of the A30 range. Unlike previous new models, which

were announced individually and at different times, the A40, A50 and A90 ranges were a new family of cars that shared a contemporary look, and gave Austin a competitive edge over its home market competitors. While the bodyshells were unique to Austin, the powerplants were destined to be shared amongst all BMC models.

The new A40 Cambridge (GS5) had an engine of identical capacity and power output (1200cc and 42bhp) of the unit previously installed in the Somerset, but the new engine was a slightly longer corporate unit, designated the BMC B-series. The Cambridge was offered initially in both two- and four-door variants, but, sadly, the two-door option was dropped after just a handful of prototypes were built.

Sharing the same bodyshell was the A50 Cambridge (HS5), which had a 1489cc 50bhp version of the same engine although, due to relatively low gearing (4.875:1), its top speed of 74mph was only marginally faster than that of the A40 Somerset it replaced.

From early 1956, Borg Warner overdrive was available on the A50, and, toward the end of its production run, it was offered with two-pedal Manumatic transmission. While the A40 Cambridge was a slow seller – just 30,666 cars finding buyers between 1954 and 1957 – almost four times as many of the bigger-engined A50 were sold, paving the way for its own replacement, the A55, a re-engineered version of the A50.

Whilst both Cambridge models had been direct replacements for the Somerset, the new A90 Westminster (BS4) replaced the A70 Hereford – and then some. In 1953, just 6008 A70 Herefords were exported to Commonwealth countries compared

The A90 Westminster got the new Nuffield-developed, 2.6 litre C-series, six cylinder engine, which it would share with its Morris rival, the Isis. (Courtesy Barry Meech)

Unlike previous new models, which were announced individually and at different times, the new A40, A50 and A90 range was a new family of cars that shared a contemporary look.

to some 44,000 Ford Zephyrs, so the new A90 was designed to provide overseas Austin dealers with a more competitive vehicle.

Visually similar in appearance to the Cambridge, albeit with a longer wheelbase and wider track, only the door pressings were common to all models and the A90 was easy to distinguish from the rear due to a horizontal rear light arrangement as distinct from the Cambridge's vertical rear light clusters.

Such was the illogical methodology at BMC that both Austin and Morris were allowed to develop and manufacture unique designs that would directly compete. The only common components were the engine and driveline, and, whereas small Morrises were now using Austin-inspired, four-cylinder engines, the new A90 would get the new Nuffield-developed, 2.6 litre C-series six cylinder engine, which it would share with the rival Morris Isis.

Prototype GS5 Cambridges had been tested with the Austin A70 engine, but vibration problems could not be eliminated until the smooth-running six unit from Nuffield was installed. Longbridge fitted the straight six with a downdraught Zenith carburettor which gave a power output of 85bhp – a substantial increase over rival six cylinder competitors from Ford (68bhp Zephyr), and Vauxhall (64bhp Velox).

Although the A90 was to remain in production for two years only (and sell in relatively small numbers compared to the more fuel-efficient A40/50), it did prove immensely popular with Britain's police forces, many of which had been using its predecessor, the A70, and appreciated the new A90's top speed of 86mph.

The A90 Westminster proved immensely popular with Britain's police forces, many of which had been using its predecessor, the A70, and appreciated the new A90's top speed of 86mph. (Courtesy Surrey police)

Sharing the same engine as the Austin-Healey 100/6, the A90 Westminster proved an ideal rally car – and a race winner. This one demonstrated that it could still hold its own at Goodwood 2008, despite rolling over in an earlier race. (Courtesy John Lakey)

The A90 was also an extremely competitive rally car, participating in a number of rallies across Europe and Africa.

For 1957 both the A50 and A90 were given a cosmetic makeover, which involved lengthening the rear end of both and the application of two-tone paintwork. The four-cylinder Cambridge became the A55 and retained the 1489cc B-series engine, developing 51bhp,

Inset, left: In 1957 the four-cylinder Cambridge became the A55 and retained the 1489cc B-series engine, developing 51bhp. (Courtesy Surrey police)

Left: There was a range-topping A105 luxury version which featured an uprated C-series twin-carburettor engine producing 102bhp (the same as the Austin-Healey 100/6).

while the Westminster became the A95 (despite still producing only 85bhp). In addition there was a range-topping A105 luxury version which featured an uprated C-series, twin-carburettor engine producing 102bhp (the same as the Austin-Healey 100/6).

The new Westminster was a glamorous car, available in a range of two-tone paint schemes. It was arguably one of the most handsome Austins ever to come out of Longbridge, two-tone styling complementing its lines much better than that of the similarly-styled Cambridge.

It was also more than a match for the rival Mk2 Ford Zephyr in terms of performance, with a top speed approaching 95mph.

In addition to a four-door saloon, Austin also used the A95 as a basis for its re-entry to the estate car market. Demand for **estate cars had been growing**

steadily during the 1950s, and, as a result, Austin approached Jensen, which was successfully building Austin-Healeys under contract, and was always keen to undertake specialist projects for Austin.

Jensen had costed out an updated metal-bodied Countryman, based on the A70 Countryman of 1953, but a deal with Austin never materialised. However, with both Standard and Hillman increasing sales of their in-house estate cars, Austin was ready to enter the market again – the resulting all-steel A95 Countryman (BW6) estate car was introduced in 1957.

Austin placed an initial order with Jensen in September 1956 for 1500 Countryman bodies. The order was subsequently extended and the last of 1998 such bodies were delivered to Longbridge in January 1959. In addition, more than 400 CKD Countryman bodies were delivered to overseas markets where local assembly was necessary because of high import duties on complete cars.

Jensen converted almost 2000 A95 Westminster bodyshells to Countryman estate cars for Austin, and they proved popular in export markets. (Courtesy Richard Calver)

Luxury cars

In the 1930s Austin had built a reputation for producing some very fine large cars, so it was no surprise when, in 1946, Len Lord announced that Austin would be building two new six-cylinder cars, with a choice of modern bodies. The Twenty Five was to be bodied at Longbridge and the other, designated the Princess, by Austin's newly-acquired coachbuilding subsidiary, Vanden Plas of Kingsbury in North London.

The new Twenty Five – following the same-style nomenclature as the Eight, Ten and Sixteen cars – was initially launched in February 1947 as the A110 Sheerline, and was Austin's first completely new post-war car, and the first to carry the legendary Flying A mascot, which Lord had stylised on the 'Winged B' of his own Bentley.

The new car was conceived as a 'poor man's

Often dubbed 'the poor man's Bentley,' the imposing A125 Sheerline was launched in 1947 using the truck-derived, six cylinder engine.

Coachbuilding at its finest! The Austin A135 Princess was built using traditional aluminium panelling over ash framing at the Kingsbury, London, works of Vanden Plas. (Courtesy Vanden Plas OC)

Bentley' but, with the 3460cc six-cylinder, truck-derived engine consuming fuel at around 15mpg, it was hardly a thrifty car. The timing of the Sheerline's launch in 1947, at the height of post-war austerity, was a bold move, though many regarded it as an ill-fated entry into a luxury car market that had virtually all but disappeared in post-war Britain ...

The more luxurious and much more stylish A120 Princess, built on the Sheerline chassis, was initially launched at the March 1947 Geneva Motor Show, and featured wood-framed, aluminium-clad Vanden Plas coachwork. Launch designations of both cars were changed almost immediately, though, when engine

capacity of the high-speed version of the contemporary truck engine was increased from 3.5 litres to 4 litres (3995cc). Overnight, the single carburettor Sheerline (DS1) became the A125 (indicating its approximate power), whilst the triple carburettor Princess became the A135 (DS2).

A long wheelbase Sheerline (DM1) appeared late in 1949, but didn't sell very well as Austin failed to appreciate the size requirements of the limousine market. Vanden Plas was initially charged with redesigning it, although the redesigned and lengthened car was ultimately clad in Princess pressings and launched as the long wheelbase DM4 Princess limousine

Above: The Austin Princess II was introduced in 1950 and featured a more cut-away rear side window to allow rear seat passengers a better view. (Courtesy Vanden Plas OC)

Below: The Austin Princess III, introduced in 1953, did away with the previous Sheerline-type grille, and the front wingline extended more horizontally into the front door. (Courtesy Vanden Plas OC)

in October 1952, ultimately replacing the long wheelbase Sheerline, which was discontinued in October 1953. The standard wheelbase Sheerline was dropped from production the following year.

The new Princess DM4 was an instant success, with the British Royal household ordering two at the 1952 London Motor Show – an order repeated three times during the model's long production run, which helped to promote the model to heads of state around the world.

The standard wheelbase models of both proved popular for weddings and with the funeral trade; the long wheelbase versions were often used as the basis for hearse and ambulance bodywork. While production of the A125 and A135s peaked at more than 3000 units in the period 1949-50, sales dropped away steadily and, by the time the DS3 Princess II was superceded by the DS5 Princes III in 1953, Princess sales had dropped to just a few hundred cars a year. In fact, the DS5, and its touring limousine counterpart, the DM5, racked up sales of just 350 vehicles between 1953 and 1956.

Throughout the 1950s Vanden Plas enjoyed the freedom to develop a number of interesting prototypes, and made a number of attempts to streamline and update the Princess design. One of the most novel

Vanden Plas was always trying new styling approaches. Sadly, this sleek Princess convertible never made it into production. (Courtesy Vanden Plas OC)

Left: The razor-edge styling of the DS7 Princess IV was a brave attempt by Vanden Plas to update the Princess in 1956. With fewer than 200 built in a three-year period, it is now one of the most sought-after of all Austin Princesses.

designs was the angular DS7 Princess IV introduced in 1956, which combined razor-edge styling with the two-tone paintwork that was all the rage at the time. Sadly, fewer than 200 saloons and touring limousine versions were sold before the model was discontinued in 1959.

While the Princess DM4 limousine was to continue in production until 1968, the late 50s witnessed a major shift away from coachbuilding techniques for the Kingsbury works. Having successfully fitted out an Austin Westminster A105 to its own high standards for the personal use of Len Lord, Vanden Plas was subsequently asked to build 500 more as a production model.

The company reacted quickly and positively to its new role of developing and refining Austin and forthcoming BMC steel-bodied cars by developing its own heavily revised versions of the new Farina-designed Austin A99 Westminster and Wolseley 6/99 saloons,

Having successfully fitted out an Austin Westminster A105 to its own high standards for the personal use of Len Lord, Vanden Plas was subsequently asked to build 500 more as a production model.

The prototype A120 which was developed into the Vanden Plas 3 litre. (Courtesy Vanden Plas OC)

it was to associate a quality car with a distinctive appearance and for it to have a 'prestige' name.

With Roland Fox's backing, John Bradley (Vanden Plas' chief designer) then quickly designed and produced the distinctive Princess front end, and, as there was insufficient time to build this into

which were announced in 1959. Prototypes of the proposed Austin A120 Vanden Plas and Wolseley 6/120 Vanden Plas were shown to Len Lord on a visit to the Kingsbury works.

However, after spending 18 months getting the project under way, Len Lord rang Roland Fox to say that he wanted to scrap the two models and convert them to a 'Princess' car. After initial thoughts of the disorganisation that this would create, Roland Fox realised that it supported what Vanden Plas had been saying for a number of years; namely, how important

a body for approval, simply superimposed it over the Westminster front end to get the Chairman's acceptance of the design.

A car was built and exhibited at the 1959 Earls Court Show and was extremely well received. Initially called the Princess 3 litre, it was renamed in 1960 the Vanden Plas Princess 3 litre when Vanden Plas became a marque in its own right. At this time the flying 'A' mascot was deleted from the DM4 Limousine and replaced with a black coronet, the 3 litre and its successors being fitted with a red coronet.

Sports cars – some were and some weren't!

Prior to the outbreak of hostilities in Europe in 1939, the nearest Austin got to building a sports car was with the lightweight 'backyard specials' constructed on the humble Austin Seven chassis. But all that was to change post-war with a new priority to sell cars in the US in order to earn export dollars.

US military personnel serving in Europe had come across sports cars for the first time whilst stationed in Britain, and many were impressed with what they saw. Len Lord wanted a piece of this potential market and so set about building Austin's most audacious post-war car – the A90 Atlantic.

The design of the car was supposedly drawn by Len Lord initially on the back of an old catalogue and passed to the Longbridge design department for further development. The process was aided by the sporty Alfa Romeo, with streamlined Pinin Farina bodywork, that turned up at Longbridge after being sold to a mystery buyer at the 1946 Geneva motor show.

Launched at the 1948 London Earl's Court Motor Show, the sleek open four-seater was the first post-war British car to dispense with a normal radiator grille. It used the chassis from the A70 Hampshire and was powered by the A70's engine bored out to produce 88bhp from 2660cc. It was one of the largest capacity four cylinder engines on the British market at the time, and, coupled with a 3.67:1 differential, gave the Atlantic convertible a top speed of close to 95mph.

Production of a hardtop coupé – branded the A90 Sports Saloon – commenced in January 1950. The

Launched in 1948, the A90 Atlantic was a futuristically-styled, two-door convertible aimed squarely at the American sports car market. (Courtesy www.stilltimecollection.co.uk)

centre section of the rear screen could be wound down for increased ventilation, and it was billed as a model for those who wanted sports car performance with saloon car comfort, although it was certainly not a sports car in the true sense, and saloon car comfort didn't extend to rear seat passengers.

To support a car that was designed from the outset for the US market, the Austin publicity machine worked overtime to demonstrate to sceptical North American car buyers that a four cylinder car could cover long distances. However, despite the A90 breaking a host of US stock car records at the Indianapolis speedway, American buyers were still few and far between and sales were disappointing. Curiously, Britain turned out to be the car's best market.

The **AUSTIN "A90"**
Atlantic Sports Saloon

The A90 Atlantic hardtop was billed as the 'Sports Saloon.'

Overall, fewer than 8000 Atlantics – both drophead and fixed head – were built between 1948-52, and just 350 went to their intended market of the US. Sadly, the Atlantic is still a much maligned model, which is a great shame as it's a superb, powerful and extremely stylish car which, when tested by *Autocar* magazine in February 1951, was described thus: "From its inception the A90 has been in a category of what may be called exciting cars."

When new, the Atlantic may have been considered an example of 'fantasy over reality;' however, today, the car is highly prized and appreciated as the style icon it really is. Even the A90's engine lives on in the Austin-Healey 100 sports car.

Even before the A90 convertible was discontinued at the end of 1950, Austin was already considering a smaller and cheaper 'sports car' based around A40 mechanicals. While the standard A40 body was not available from the UK factory as a convertible, a number of open-topped Tourers were built by local assemblers in Australia. Yet, when the Longbridge-sanctioned convertible A40 finally came into being, it was almost by accident.

Independent car builder Jensen was planning a large sports touring car, and sent a delegation to Longbridge in the summer of 1949 to negotiate a deal to source a supply of A70 chassis and Sheerline six cylinder engines for its planned Jensen Interceptor. Jensen got the deal,

While the A90 Atlantic may not have been the sales success that Leonard Lord had hoped for, today, the cars are highly prized as the style icons they are.

but only on condition that it designed a small sports car for Austin, too.

In order to meet the tight deadline imposed by Len Lord, Jensen's designer, Eric Neale, drew heavily on the Interceptor concept; the resultant design got the seal of approval from Austin and Jensen got an order to build, trim and paint the bodies. After a small number of prototypes were produced, Jensen won an order to build more than 3000 of the new car, which was to be known as the A40 Sports. The cars were assembled by Jensen and the aluminium-panelled bodies were painted, trimmed and mounted on chassis sent from Longbridge.

The A40 Sports was launched at the Earls Court Motor Show in October 1950 to favourable public reaction. The car certainly looked sleek, stylish and sporty, but even with twin SU carburettors and larger

The Jensen-designed A40 Sports took styling cues from its big brother, the Jensen Interceptor. (Courtesy Nic Cooper)

The stylish A40 Sports was built between 1950 and 1953, during which time more than 4200 were assembled by Jensen. At some stage this example has acquired non-standard wheels from an A40 saloon.

Austin's newly-acquired coachbuilder, Vanden Plas of London, was given the task of building a hard top for the A40 Sports. (Courtesy Vanden Plas OC)

inlet valves boosting the 1200cc engine from 42 to 46bhp, including 'Sports' in its name was something of misnomer.

Production of both the GD2 A40 Sports and the later GD3 version with column-mounted gear lever and revised instruments, reached a total of more than 4200 units before the model was withdrawn in 1953. Jensen had hoped that there would be a Jensen-built replacement for the A40 Sports, and had even developed a prototype which it intended to have ready in time for the 1952 Motor Show, but supplier problems delayed its timely completion.

However, before it could be shown to Austin management, Len Lord struck a deal with Donald Healey to build the Austin-Healey 100. Not to be outdone, Jensen offered to build the Healey and won the contract. So, while Jensen did not get the order to build the Somerset dhc (which went instead to Carbodies), by then it had a more prestigious order from Austin – to build a real sports car!

The first real sports car

The Earls Court Motor Show of 1952 saw the debut of Donald Healey's 100 sports car, which used many of the A90 Atlantic's mechanical components. On the opening day of the show only two Healey 100s actually existed; one undertaking a high speed run at Jabekke in Belgium and the other on the show stand. Despite these small production 'technicalities' American dealers were placing orders for 500 or more, and wanted to know when they could take delivery.

It wasn't long before Austin's own dealers were also asking for the car in large numbers, so Lord decided that it would make sound business sense to change the name of the car to the Austin-Healey 100. Overnight, the Healey stand was completely refurbished and rebranded: it is believed that this is the only time that a car changed its brand name at the Motor Show.

Lord had clearly backed a winner and, for the first time, Austin had a car that could justify its 'sports car' tag. Volume production of the 100 was awarded to Jensen, which initially built a small batch of BN1 aluminium bodies to specifications laid down by Healey. However, the size of the Carters Green factory was becoming a limiting factor in the production of Austin-Healey bodies, and so, feeling secure in terms of Austin orders, the Jensen brothers found a bigger site in West Bromwich where a new factory was built at Kelvin Way.

Whilst the A90 Atlantic clocked up a number of impressive endurance records which didn't help sales, the Austin-Healey produced no end of new speed records that proved it was a sports car with a capital 'S.' The 90bhp standard car was advertised with a claimed 0-60mph time of 10.5 seconds, and in 1954 Donald Healey achieved almost 193mph over a flying kilometre in a 224bhp supercharged and streamlined 100. Then Carroll Shelby went on to break 16 US and international speed records at averages of nearly 160mph. Record and race achievements resulted in the production of the special 100S (Sebring) model, of which just 50 were built.

Production commenced at Jensen's new West Bromwich factory in 1955, just in time for the launch of the BN2 model, which featured a new Austin four-speed overdrive gearbox with central gear lever. The model was relatively short-lived, replaced in August 1956 by the even more powerful six cylinder 100/6 using the 102bhp BMC C-series engine from the Austin A105. In

Launched in 1952, the Austin-Healey 100 was the first real sports car to wear the Austin badge. Power came from the A90 Atlantic's 2.6 litre, four cylinder engine.

a little over three years, 14,600 Austin-Healey 100s were produced, just 10 per cent of which were built with rhd and just 3.5 per cent of the overall total were 'home market' cars.

In 1957 engine power was increased to 117bhp by the addition of a six port cylinder head, which gave much improved performance. In April 1958 the BN6 version of the car was introduced, this time featuring 2-seater bodywork, although it still retained the longer wheelbase. Production figures were 10,268 for the 2+2

100/6 (BN4) and 4150 for the 2-seater 100/6 (BN6). Production ended with the introduction of the Austin-Healey 3000 in June 1959.

Despite the A40 Sports' failure to create a market for small sports cars, the concept of a small open sportster was never far from the minds of Austin's engineers. An ill-fated prototype A30 convertible was built in 1951, but never went into production. Then, in 1953, ideas were nurtured again at Longbridge to produce an A30 Sports, including the possibility of a

The new 100/6 (BN4) looked similar to the 100 and had a lengthened wheelbase to accommodate occasional rear seats.

space-frame and fibreglass-bodied car. A lone prototype was built, though in the end it was decided that fibreglass was not an option for an 'Austin.'

However, Len Lord was still keen to pursue the concept of a small and affordable sportster to buck the trend whereby sports cars continued to get bigger and be more expensive. During a conversation with Donald Healey in 1956, the two men discovered that they had been thinking along the same lines ...

Healey was given the run of the BMC parts bin, and used a combination of A35 and Morris Minor mechanical parts to come up with a design proposal for

The 100/6 was a huge sales success in the US, and helped Austin reclaim some of the status it achieved when it first launched the humble A40 in North America.

an A-series-engined sports car. Dubbed the Austin-Healey Sprite, it was a cheap, simple sports car which would have mass appeal, particularly to young American drivers.

Launched in 1958 with a twin carburettor 948cc engine producing 43bhp, the Sprite was built by MG at Abingdon. This budget sports car was slightly impractical, without a boot lid and with a one-piece front end that was prone to accident damage, but its cuteness won the day and the car turned out to be huge success with more than 48,000 built in the first four years.

The Metropolitan

U nder pressure from the 'Big Three' American auto makers, Nash looked towards the smaller, more economical end of the US car market in the early 1950s. Based on the success of its 'mid-size' Rambler – launched in 1950 – Nash decided to press ahead with the design of small car.

A prototype was conceived that minimised tooling, to enable door pressings to be used on either side of the car, and front and rear diagonally-opposed wings to be formed from the same press. Dubbed the 'Metropolitan,' the car was supposedly aimed at American women. However, in order to develop the Metropolitan without incurring tooling-up costs (which were prohibitively high for a small independent car maker), Nash negotiated a contract in 1952 whereby Austin would build the cars in Britain while Nash held exclusive marketing rights.

The Longbridge-built Metropolitan was launched in the US in 1954, and early examples were badge-engineered as Nash and Hudson brands.

Fisher & Ludlow, which Austin was about to take over, was contracted to build the bodies.

The underpinnings of the Metropolitan were designed around A30 and A40 mechanicals to take full advantage of Austin's knowledge and experience in building 'small' cars. Compared with Austin's home market cars, the range of colours chosen by Nash was exceedingly bold, but may have ultimately influenced Longbridge to 'brighten up' its own range.

Production cars began rolling off Longbridge assembly lines in the autumn of 1953, and some 3000 were shipped to North America in preparation for the model's launch in spring 1954. Austin was proud to have been associated with the project, which it considered to be the first economy car built in Britain and designed in America for American drivers.

When Nash merged with Hudson in 1954 to form American Motors Corporation (AMC), a 'Hudson' branded version of the Metropolitan was added to the range. When the Nash and Hudson names were eventually phased out by AMC, the Metropolitan became a brand in its own right.

The 'Met' originally used the 1200cc motor from the A40, but this was replaced by the new B-series 1489cc engine in 1956. An opening boot lid was finally added in 1959. While some 104,377 Metropolitans were built between 1953 and 1961, it is open to speculation whether or not the car could have been more successful if it had been marketed properly. It appears that, apart from launch publicity in 1954, the first national

The Austin Metropolitan was finally launched in the UK in 1957, although the car was never to carry any Austin badges.

advertising campaign for the Metropolitan did not take place in the US until 1960. While strikes in the UK made the Americans a little nervous of promoting a car that Longbridge maybe couldn't deliver, it seems that after the death of George Mason, president of Nash Kelvinator – who had been instrumental in the Met's development and building in the UK – the new management did not have the same passion for a small economical car. Another problem during the mid-50s was that Nash dealers were reluctant to push an 'imported' car over the home-grown product.

Rather late in the Metropolitan's production life, it was earmarked for sale by Austin in Australia. Curiously, the Australian *Motor Manual* of June 1957, pondering on what new Austin-derived models could be introduced down-under as all-Australian BMC cars, noted the Metropolitan's sales success in the US. It speculated that a four-door version was going into production, and was expected to be sold in Australia. Now, wouldn't that be something ...

Taxicabs

Austin joined the London cab trade in the late 1920s, and enjoyed market dominance with its modified Heavy 12/4 chassis, which was sold by Mann & Overton, London's largest and longest-running taxi dealership, with bodywork constructed by numerous coachbuilders. However, with the outbreak of WWII, Austin ceased production of the model.

Austin's old rival, Nuffield, built a prototype of a new Oxford taxi in 1940 and ran it throughout the war. It was eventually passed by the Public Carriage Office for use in London in 1946, and Nuffield put it into production the following year, allowing taxi dealership Beardmores of Hendon to sell the new cab to taxi fleets decimated by wartime bombing. This put Mann & Overton in a desperate situation if it wanted to retain market dominance.

Mann & Overton wanted a new post-war taxicab with modern all-steel bodywork. Austin initially offered a modified version of its pre-war chassis, with a new 14 horsepower ohv engine. This was designated the Austin FX and Mann & Overton began testing this chassis fitted

Top right: Launched in 1948, the FX3 retained the half-width driver's cab to allow bulky items of luggage to be carried in the open space alongside the driver. It remained in production until 1958.

The FL1 hire car variant was launched at the same time as the FX3 and had a full-width driver's compartment, complete with nearside front passenger door. (Courtesy James Platt)

FX3-based shooting brake with bodywork by Whitacres of Stoke-on-Trent.

with a body taken from one of its old cabs. However, the modified chassis and new engine proved woefully inadequate.

Clearly valuing the taxicab market, Austin set about constructing a new purpose-built chassis, designated the FX2, which was stronger yet conventional in design, and engineered it to take a brand new overhead valve, 2199cc engine which it had launched in the Austin Sixteen.

With Austin now back in the frame for the supply of chassis, Mann & Overton struck a deal with Carbodies of Coventry, whereby the cost of tooling for the new

body was split between Carbodies, Mann & Overton and Austin. After testing of the prototype FX2, Austin's position as a major builder of taxicabs that met the tough regulations laid down by London's Metropolitan Police was assured in June 1948 with the launch of a slightly modified version, designated the FX3.

As with previous purpose-built taxicabs, the FX3 had a half-width driver's cab to allow for bulky luggage items to be carried on the open space alongside the driver. It was also the first 'enclosed driver' cab, with a sliding glass partition to the driver's left.

The FL1 hire car variant was launched at the same

FL1-based ice cream van.

time, and this had a full width driver's compartment, complete with a nearside front passenger door. Intended from the outset to capitalise on the investment in tooling by Austin and Mann & Overton, the FL1 was a slow seller compared to its taxicab sibling. Whereas the FX3 was free of purchase tax after 1953, the FL1 was never type-approved by the Public Carriage Office, so couldn't be considered either a cab or a commercial vehicle and attracted purchase tax for its entire production life.

When Austin and Morris combined to form the British Motor Corporation in 1952, Mann & Overton and BMC found themselves in the enviable situation of having somewhat of a monopoly in the taxicab market. Despite now being head of both Austin and Morris, Len Lord was a staunch 'Austin' man and so axed production of the older-designed Oxford cab. However the following year, something even more radical was to affect cab production.

In 1953, diesel oil was subject to low taxation in Britain, and was therefore about half the price of petrol, which prompted a London-based engineering company to install a 1.8 litre Borgward diesel in an FX3. While the small diesel made the cab very slow, it did return much better fuel economy, which prompted other companies to offer retrofits of a variety of diesels ranging from the Standard Vanguard's Ferguson tractor-based engine to diesels from Mercedes-Benz and Perkins.

The Standard engine proved the most popular with some taxi companies converting their entire fleet, but it didn't sit well with Austin to have its engines replaced by those from a rival. So Austin launched its own diesel-engined FX3 in 1954 with a unit developed from the 2.2 litre petrol engine. Despite teething problems with early engines, diesels proved their worth; by 1955, 90 per cent of new FX3s were diesel-powered.

All production bodies for the FX3 and FL1 were built by Carbodies of Coventry and, in addition, a chassis/scuttle was also available and proved popular for specialist applications. The versatility of the 25ft turning circle meant many chassis were bodied as delivery vans for London newspaper groups – some even ended up as service vans, ice creams vans, and even wooden-bodied shooting brakes.

In addition to plying for hire trade in the towns and cities of Britain, Austin had originally envisaged the FX3 operating in export markets, and left-hand drive versions had been demonstrated in Canada in 1950. In addition, an FX3 was trialled in New York, where, despite gaining public acceptance, it was not well received by cab drivers used to bigger and more powerful home-built machinery – a situation that was proving all too familiar for Austin in North America. However, the FX3 did enjoy some success in Europe where 500 were exported to Spain, with the majority going to Madrid.

Production of the FX3 ended in 1958 after 7267 had been built, but work on its replacement had begun in 1956 when Eric Bailey, who had just finished his work on the Metropolitan, was asked to design a new Austin cab. Eric had also worked at Vanden Plas and so incorporated bodylines which allowed for the possibility of using contemporary two-tone paint schemes.

The new model, which was revealed to the cab

FX4s awaiting fares at London's King Cross station. (Copyright English Heritage/NMR)

trade in 1958, was designed to have a ten-year lifespan, but who would have guessed that it would become one of the longest running and most widely recognised British icons of all time?

The FX4 came with the BMC 2.2 litre diesel engine as standard, mated to a Borg-Warner automatic transmission, and its chassis was updated with the suspension and rear axle from the A90 Westminster. There were initial teething problems with pressing such large roof sections in one piece and also with the complicated shape of the bonnet. However, these were ironed out very quickly by Carbodies, earning it the reputation of being amongst the best 'metal bashers' in Britain.

The FX4 was revealed to the cab trade in 1958. Designed to have a ten-year lifespan, who would have guessed that it would become one of the longest-running and most widely recognised British icons of all time?

Off-roaders

Austin's impressive wartime vehicle production had forged strong links with Britain's military, particularly army top brass. Keen to win further army contracts – whilst acutely aware of the success of the ubiquitous Jeep – Austin was anxious to develop its own general purpose 4x4, and the British army was keen to have it.

Austin had worked on plans for a general purpose 4x4 during WWII, but, despite this, it was rival Nuffield that was first to conduct prototype trials with the British Army. However, whilst this resulted in Wolseley being contracted to build 12 further prototypes, it was actually Austin that was awarded the contract for continued development of these prototypes into what was officially known as the Truck ¼ ton 4x4 CT. Austin named this the Champ and the British Army adopted the name.

The army initially ordered 15,000 Champs in August 1951, but the terms of the contract were altered many times. Champs were designed to a very high standard and specification, which may ultimately have been their undoing.

They could operate underwater and their unique gearboxes gave them five speeds in both forward and reverse. They had excellent on and off-road capabilities and, while some early examples had been fitted with the 2.6 litre engine from the A90 Atlantic, series production versions were equipped with the powerful 2.8 litre Rolls-Royce B40 four cylinder engine manufactured under licence by Austin, the Champ was limited to 60mph for stability and could return more than 15mpg, although troops tried hard to reduce this to below 10mpg.

Above: The Champ had excellent on- and off-road capabilities and, while some early examples were fitted with the 2.6 litre engine from the A90 Atlantic, series production versions were equipped with the powerful 2.8 litre, Rolls-Royce B40 four cylinder engine manufactured under licence by Austin.

The Champ was limited to 60mph for reasons of stability, and could return more than 15mpg, although troops tried hard to get this down to below 10mpg!

The short wheelbase Gipsy used the same BMC 2.2 litre diesel engine as the larger long wheelbase version; both were well-received by a range of private and government-run organisations.

Although the Gipsy looked like a Land-Rover, its bodywork was pressed steel and the harsh conditions in which it frequently operated resulted in serious rust problems.

When the Champ was first introduced the Land-Rover was already four years old. Whilst it was yet to acquire its world-famous reputation, the War Office purchased more than 2000 Land-Rovers between 1948 and 1952 which, although suitable for military use, a stronger body and more powerful engine was wanted by army chiefs, and this was delivered in the shape of the new 86 inch wheelbase Land-Rover. The new Land-Rovers cost less than half the price of a Champ, but the extra cost of the Austin was justified on the grounds of the purpose-built off-roader's high quality. However, Champ orders were cut in favour of Land-Rovers and, by the time Champ production ceased in 1956, almost 12,000 had been built in a variety of configurations to suit a wide range of military applications.

Jensen had ultimately missed out on lucrative contract work to build bodies for the Champ, but the West Bromwich-based company fared a little better when it became involved in building special bodies for the Austin Gipsy – Austin's Land-Rover clone. This new off-roader picked up where the complex and expensive Champ 4x4 had left off, and was essentially built to a standard that would enable Austin to compete for lucrative Government contracts.

Power for the Gipsy came from the ubiquitous BMC 2.2 litre diesel engine. Whilst the Gipsy *looked* like a Land-Rover, its bodywork was pressed from steel – unlike the 'Landy' which had aluminium bodywork – and the harsh conditions that such vehicles frequently operated in resulted in severe rust problems. The Gipsy was well received by public and private buyers alike, and versions were constructed for a wide variety of applications, including fire, police and ambulance services. However, none ever found their way into British military use, largely because of the Gipsy's propensity to rust.

Approximately 21,000 Austin Gipsys, of both short and long wheelbase configurations, were built in the ten-year period before production was terminated in 1968, when BMC merged with Leyland and then focused all of its marketing efforts on the Leyland-owned Land-Rover.

Light commercials

One of the priorities at the end of WWII was to rebuild Britain, and vehicle manufacturers paid special attention to producing light commercials that could assist in this task. Both the Eight and Ten horsepower chassis became available as vans, with capacities of 6cwt and 10cwt respectively, but Austin knew there was a need for a vehicle that bridged the gap between these small vans and its K-series heavy trucks, which had first been introduced in 1939.

Austin introduced its K8 Three-Way-Loader van in 1946 with bodywork by Carbodies. (Courtesy www.stilltimecollection.co.uk)

The solution was the forward-control, K8 series 25cwt van introduced in 1946, and powered by the lusty four cylinder Sixteen engine rated at 65bhp. The 300cu ft steel body had doors on both sides, as well as at the rear, and was given the name of Three-Way-Loader.

As a result of Austin's wartime connection with Carbodies, the Coventry coachbuilder was asked to build the bodies for the K8. This was a far cry from the elegant drophead coupés that Carbodies had produced in the 1930s, but any work was good work in the early post-war years.

Building the Three-Way-Loader bodies brought together old and new construction methods, with a pressed steel cab joined to a wood-framed body clad in aluminium sheets.

The K8 was a big and versatile van, its appearance more modern and stylish than that of its rivals from Commer and Morris. The K8 was also offered as a chassis with, or without, a cab, and a number were bodied as trucks, coaches and ambulances. A total of 27,000 K8s were built during the model's seven year production run, with output at its highest between 1948 and 1951.

An A40 Devon-based van followed the K8 into

Above: An early 40 pickup with chrome grille. (Courtesy www.stilltimecollection.co.uk)

British Railways had a large fleet of A40 vans. This example is being used for driver training duties. (Courtesy www. stilltimecollection. co.uk)

The most stylish A40 pickup was the Australian Larke Hoskins Hi-Lite, which featured rear bodywork moulded into the cab, plus a Perspex wraparound rear window.

The A40 pickup lent itself to many roles. This industrial fire truck was retired from UK service and is now part of Rob Stuart's amazing Austin collection in California.

production in 1947, and hot on its heels in 1948 was a pickup truck version. Both proved so popular that when the A40 Devon car ceased production in February 1952, the Devon-based van, pickup and Countryman models continued until 1957.

The A40 commercials initially used the same front panels as the car, but a new pressed steel radiator grille replaced the chrome car-style grille in 1951, and the original 1200cc A40 engine was replaced by the new BMC B-series 1200cc unit in 1954. A uniquely Australian pickup was the Coupé Utility, often referred to as an 'ute, and a number of Australian bodybuilders produced such pickup bodies, although the most stylish was the Larke Hoskins Hi-Lite, which featured rear bodywork moulded into the cab, plus a Perspex wrap-around rear window.

Another company seeking to win post-war contract work from Austin was Jensen Motors, which picked up its first order in 1948. Longbridge initially ordered 24 pickup van bodies on the K8 25cwt chassis, followed by an order for a further 150. On completion of the special K8 bodies, Jensen was then asked to build five pickup bodies on the new A70 Hampshire chassis. Austin had especially lengthened the A70 chassis and fitted larger brakes and wheels to enable it to take special bodies.

The five pickup bodies were the first of an order for 1000 such bodies built by Jensen to enable Austin to offer a 'factory-built' pickup, which was designated the BQU2. These were far from elaborate bodies with the first order costed out at £18 each; by the time a fifth and final order was placed, unit prices had fallen as low as £8 per body.

The A70 pickup had a load capacity of 15cwt and was intended to be a rugged, no frills workhorse equally suitable for life on the farm or the dirt tracks of Africa or Australia. It also proved popular as a garage service vehicle which could not only carry a mechanic's tools, but also tow in a vehicle for repair if need be.

The Earls Court Motor Show of October 1950 saw the A70 Hampshire superceded by an updated A70 – the Hereford. The saloon had a wheelbase three inches longer than the car it replaced and, as before, Austin introduced a long wheelbase light commercial chassis. It had a more streamlined pickup body, built by Briggs of Dagenham, which featured a design integral to the front of the car.

More than 20,000 A70 pickups were built between 1950 and 1954.

The A70 Hampshire pickup proved particularly popular in Australia and New Zealand. (Courtesy Richard Calver)

The A70 chassis cab was a versatile workhorse and could be bodied to fulfil varied roles, such as a milk truck.

While car designs were constantly changed and upgraded, Austin never quite saw the need to apply the same thinking to its light commercial range and, by the mid-1950s, its products were looking a little tired. Production of the big pickups had ended in 1954 when the A70 Hereford ceased production; by 1957 when the last few A40s were built, the design was ten years old.

While no commercial versions of the new A50 were built in the UK, the Australian-assembled A50 'ute was light years ahead of the Devon-based A40 version, which must have influenced the Longbridge-built A55 10cwt van and pickup launched in 1958.

This A70 Hereford-based chassis cab was fitted with a tilt-body for farmwork.

This A70 truck sports most unusual bodywork, having been converted from a pickup to a box van for the delivery of newspapers. (Courtesy www.stilltimecollection.co.uk)

The 25ft turning circle of the FX3 taxicab chassis made it well-suited to newspaper delivery van duties in London. Note the sliding door for quick entry. (Courtesy Bill Munro)

The A55 had a useful 96cu ft carrying capacity, and was more modern and more stylish than its nearest rival, the Commer Express delivery van. Curiously, its launch came some six years after Austin had merged with Morris, and yet BMC still did not enjoy any initial economies of scale by allowing the new Austin to be built completely separate to the Morris Oxford pickup.

While most Austin light commercials from the early and mid-50s were designed on uniquely Austin-based vehicles, BMC was slowly rationalising its range by focusing on BMC-derived models. The 15cwt J2 launched in 1956 was BMC's first unitary-construction

Although a number of FX4 newspaper delivery vans were supplied to national newspaper groups, off-the-shelf vans like the ubiquitous Bedford CA were slowly gaining ground on the purpose-built specials. (Courtesy www.stilltimecollection.co.uk)

The A55 10cwt van and pickup was launched in 1958. It had a useful 96cu ft carrying capacity and was more modern and more stylish than its nearest rival, the Commer Express delivery van. (Courtesy www.stilltimecollection.co.uk)

The 15cwt Austin J2, launched in 1956, was BMC's first unitary-construction van, and was also produced in pickup, minibus and chassis-cab derivatives. (Courtesy www.stilltimecollection.co.uk)

van, and was also produced in pickup, minibus and chassis-cab derivatives. The Austin J2 was powered by the 1489cc B-series engine, mounted underfloor alongside the driver; a diesel-powered version was later introduced and this proved a tough workhorse, although somewhat slow and noisy.

Left: The A35 van superceded the A30 in 1956, and remained in production well into the late 1960s.

The Austin J2 van proved extremely popular as the basis of an armoured security van for Securicor, and was, at one time, seen on every High Street across Britain. (Courtesy BMC J2/152 Register)

The BMC influence

When Leonard Lord masterminded the merger with Nuffield in 1952 to form the British Motor Corporation (BMC), he brought together the skills, expertise and brands of Austin, Morris, MG, Riley and Wolseley to create the fourth largest motor company in the world, and it was completely logical that he should quickly take over as chairman of BMC.

As an ex-Nuffield man himself, Lord had constantly fuelled the rivalry between Austin and Nuffield, and so knew very well that Austin and Morris were deep-seated rivals, if not actually enemies. Lord was originally employed at Wolseley, working his way up to MD of Morris before quitting to join Austin in 1936. It was an acrimonious departure and Lord is often quoted as stating that he would: "Take Cowley apart, brick by bloody brick," which didn't sit well with Lord Nuffield, or the men at Cowley, and the animosity it created seriously hampered the on-off negotiations of the two rivals prior to the 1952 merger. Even after the merger Longbridge men considered Cowley men to be the sworn enemy.

The formation of BMC didn't lead immediately to any great rationalisation of products or dealers; in fact, throughout the 1950s the group pursued a policy that maintained marque names and associated dealer networks. Engineering was one of the few areas where product-sharing was introduced, with the notable example of the new 803cc A-series engine developed for the A30 and installed in the Morris Minor.

The new BMC B-series, 1489cc four cylinder engine became the standard unit for all group family saloons by the mid-50s, and the Nuffield-designed, 2.6 litre six cylinder engine not only found its way into the big Morrises, Wolseleys and Rileys for which it was originally intended, but also the A90 Westminster and Austin-Healey 100/6.

Although engines were standardised by the mid-50s, common body styles and designs were still years away, and with all BMC design work now centered on the Austin drawing office at Longbridge, many Cowley men felt that, when it came to new models, there was a strong bias toward Austin. That new models such as the Austin Gipsy, Austin A40 Farina and Austin-Healey Sprite were to have no Morris equivalents must have gone some way to underscoring that feeling, and the

The new BMC B-series, 1489cc four cylinder engine became the standard power unit for all group family saloons by the mid-50s, including the A55 Cambridge.

Based on the Austin A95 Westminster, Morris Marshall saloons and Traveller estate cars were built by BMC in Australia to give Nuffield dealerships a six cylinder product to sell once the Isis had been discontinued. (Courtesy Richard Calver)

fact that profits from selling Morris cars were used to modernise Austin production lines at Longbridge must have gone down like a lead balloon at Cowley.

During the mid-1950s the Austin range was constantly upgraded or given face-lifts, but the mid-range Cowley and Oxford saloons were looking decidedly 'old school' and sales suffered accordingly. Even the six cylinder Isis could not match the flamboyance of the A95 Westminster and was to be the last six cylinder Morris saloon produced for the home market for more than a decade.

The rivalry between Austin and Morris also impacted on BMC's export operations, such as the lucrative Australian market where BMC Australia was never allowed to forget that it was a subsidiary of a British firm, whose main function was to buy from Britain and sell locally. This policy meant that the Australian management was constantly at loggerheads with Longbridge about having models that were less than ideal for local market conditions – a strategy that eventually led to the mighty BMC empire disappearing from the Australian market in 1974 – but that's another story ...

Whilst Nuffield had been the dominant partner in Australia at the time BMC was formed, Morris sales had fallen into decline by the mid-50s, compared with those of Austin. Driving conditions and distances travelled in Australia were vastly different to those in Britain, and local car-buying trends created a healthy market for small capacity, six cylinder cars, known locally as 'light sixes.'

GM's Holden FJ light six, introduced in 1953, quickly became the top selling car in Australia, and was much cheaper than the locally-assembled A70 Hereford or later A90 Westminster. By the time the A95 Westminster was launched, Nuffield dealers were having a hard time as the Cowley, Oxford and Isis were considered unexciting – even stodgy by some local critics.

Even in the late 50s BMC dealers in Australia were still staunchly divided between Austin and Nuffield camps, and following the demise of the six cylinder Morris Isis, the Morris Marshall was created by BMC in Australia to give Nuffield dealers something to sell in the large family car sector. The car was, of course, an Austin A95 Westminster that had received bizarre cosmetic surgery.

Available as both a four-door saloon and an estate car known as the Traveller, the Marshall first appeared in Australia in 1957, technically the largest Morris ever sold in that country. However, the car was never a big seller

Eager to maintain the flow of new models in Australia, BMC took the Wolseley 1500 bodyshell and created both Morris and Austin versions. The resulting Austin Lancer used the 1489cc B-series engine. (Courtesy Ron Short)

and therefore not a commercial success. Out of 11,626 Morris cars sold in Australia in 1959, just 369 were Marshalls; its high price tag meant it couldn't compete against the market-leading Holden FC.

Another uniquely Australian Austin was the Lancer, introduced in April 1958 alongside its Morris Major sibling. Despite wanting to take the fight to Holden in the light six market, BMC Australia was once again forced to take a concept that worked well on the British home market and make the best of it!

Rumours abounded in the Australian motoring press in the mid-50s about some great new cars from BMC, possibly powered by the stalwart A70 engine. It was suggested that there was even a four-door version of the

Metropolitan, though in reality the new car couldn't have been more different from any of these.

While the Wolseley 1500 bodyshell on which the Lancer was based was a refreshing combination of a relatively large engine in a car of modest proportions, it was hardly the new light six saloon that Austin desperately needed to stay competitive.

Eager to prove the performance of the Lancer, BMC became a silent partner in Australian motor sport, and encouraged its Austin dealers to enter competitions to generate publicity. Therefore, two Austin Lancers were factory-built for road racing in 1958; one with an MGA twin-cam motor (the first of its type to reach Australia), and the other fitted with an alloy HRG Derrington head,

In 1958, two Austin Lancers were factory-built in Australia for road racing: one with an MGA twin-cam motor and the other fitted with an alloy HRG Derrington head. The latter car (seen here) had a top speed of well over 100mph, and was capable of running the standing quarter mile in 17.05 seconds. (Courtesy *North Daily Leader*)

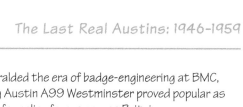

Farina styling heralded the era of badge-engineering at BMC, and the resulting Austin A99 Westminster proved popular as the car of choice for police forces across Britain. (Courtesy Police Vehicle Enthusiasts Club)

Introduced in December 1958, the bodyshell and running gear of the Pinin Farina-designed Austin A55 Cambridge was shared by Morris, MG, Riley, and Wolseley marques, in addition to Austin.

complete with all the MG go-faster bits. The latter had a top speed of well over 100mph, and was capable of running the standing quarter mile in 17.05 seconds.

The two works racers went extremely well, with Brian Foley driving the Derrington car to seven class wins out of eight races. Both cars were sold off when the Series 2 Lancers appeared, and Wayne Thompson was lucky enough to acquire the Derrington car in August 1959 from Leaton Motors, which he still owns – and occasionally races – today. Sadly, the twin-cam car has long since disappeared and rumour has it that its engine ended up in a power boat.

As the 1950s drew to a close, BMC's stranglehold grew ever stronger at Austin. With the introduction of the Farina-styled A55 Cambridge in December 1958, the A99 Westminster in 1959, and the front-wheel-drive Mini in the same year, Longbridge was about to head off in a totally new direction ...

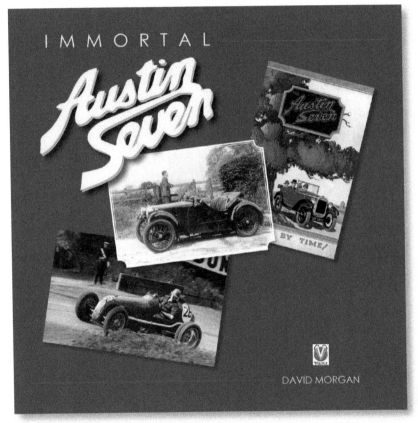

"Immortal Austin Seven" tells the story of this most popular of prewar cars in all its variations from the earliest Chummy of the 1920s through Sports, Military, Box and Ruby Saloons to the exquisite Twin Cam racers of the late 1930s. The book includes period, detail drawings and rarely seen photographs – a must for the Austin Seven enthusiast.

ISBN: 978-1-845849-79-5
Hardback • 24.8x24.8cm • 228 pages • 319 colour and b&w pictures

For more info on Veloce titles, visit our website at www.veloce.co.uk
email info@veloce.co.uk • tel: +44 (0)1305 260068

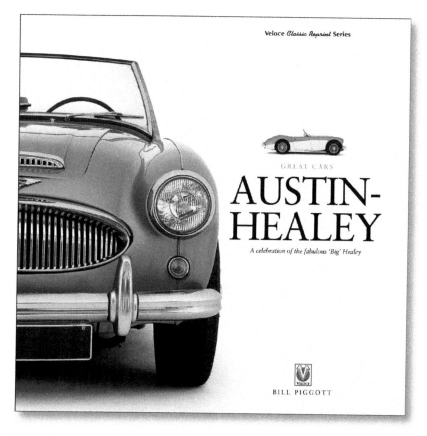

The Austin Healey – or 'Big' Healey – is one of the iconic British sports cars. The first Austin-Healey 100 model was unveiled at the 1952 Earls Court Motor Show, and when the last car rolled off the production line in 1967, over 73,000 examples had been built.

ISBN: 978-1-845848-55-2
Hardback • 25x25cm • 160 pages • 270 pictures

For more info on Veloce titles, visit our website at www.veloce.co.uk
email info@veloce.co.uk • tel: +44 (0)1305 260068

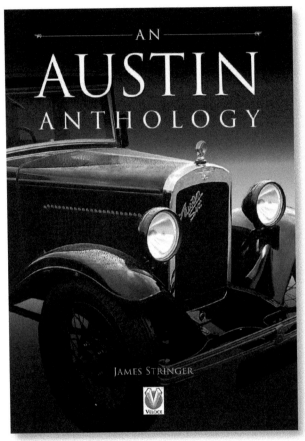

An engaging collection of short stories featuring some of the more unusual products that came out of Longbridge, such as the 40hp motorcar, probably the first motor home ever built, and the bi-plane small enough to keep in your garage.

ISBN: 978-1-787111-91-2
Hardback • 21x14.8cm • 112 pages • 109 b&w pictures

For more info on Veloce titles, visit our website at www.veloce.co.uk
email info@veloce.co.uk • tel: +44 (0)1305 260068

More *Those were the days ...* **titles from Veloce Publishing –**

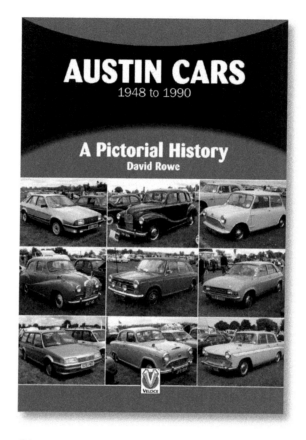

A full-colour comprehensive guide to all Austin cars built from 1948 until the end of production in the 1990s, with an informative history, detailed model-by-model comparisons and technical information.

ISBN: 978-1-787112-19-3
Paperback • 21x14.8cm • 112 pages • 280 pictures

For more info on Veloce titles, visit our website at www.veloce.co.uk
email info@veloce.co.uk • tel: +44 (0)1305 260068

Also from Veloce Publishing –

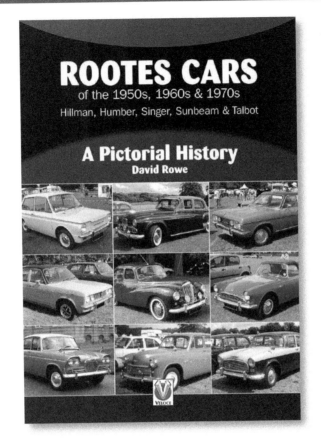

Rootes Cars of the '50s,' 60s & '70s is the only full-colour comprehensive guide to all Hillman, Humber, Sunbeam, Singer & Talbot cars & vans, built from 1950 until the end of production in the 1970s. With model-by-model descriptions and detailed technical information, this is an invaluable Rootes resource.

ISBN: 978-1-845849-93-1
Paperback • 21x14.8cm • 168 pages • 1083 colour and b&w pictures

For more info on Veloce titles, visit our website at www.veloce.co.uk
email info@veloce.co.uk • tel: +44 (0)1305 260068

Index